For Christopher

It is not wise to allow children to eat
raw cake mix. The raw ingredients can
cause stomach upsets.

First paperback edition 1997

A CIP catalogue record for this book is available
from the British Library.
ISBN 0-7136-4788-4

First published 1990 in hardback by A & C Black (Publishers) Ltd, 35 Bedford Row, London WC1R 4JH
© 1990, 1997 A & C Black (Publishers) Ltd

Photographs © 1990, 1997 Fiona Pragoff

Acknowledgements
Edited by Barbara Taylor
Science consultant Dr Bryson Gore
Illustrations by Alex Ayliffe

The photographer, authors and publishers would like
to thank the following people whose help and
co-operation made this book possible: Peter,
Stuart, Radwa, Katie and their parents.
The staff and pupils at St George's School.

Typeset by Spectrum Typesetting, London
Printed in Singapore by Tien Wah Press (Pte.) Ltd

My Cake

Sheila Gore
Photographs by Fiona Pragoff

A & C Black · London

It's my birthday!
All these things are
for my party.

I'm going to make my own birthday cake.

The recipe tells me how much
I need of each thing.

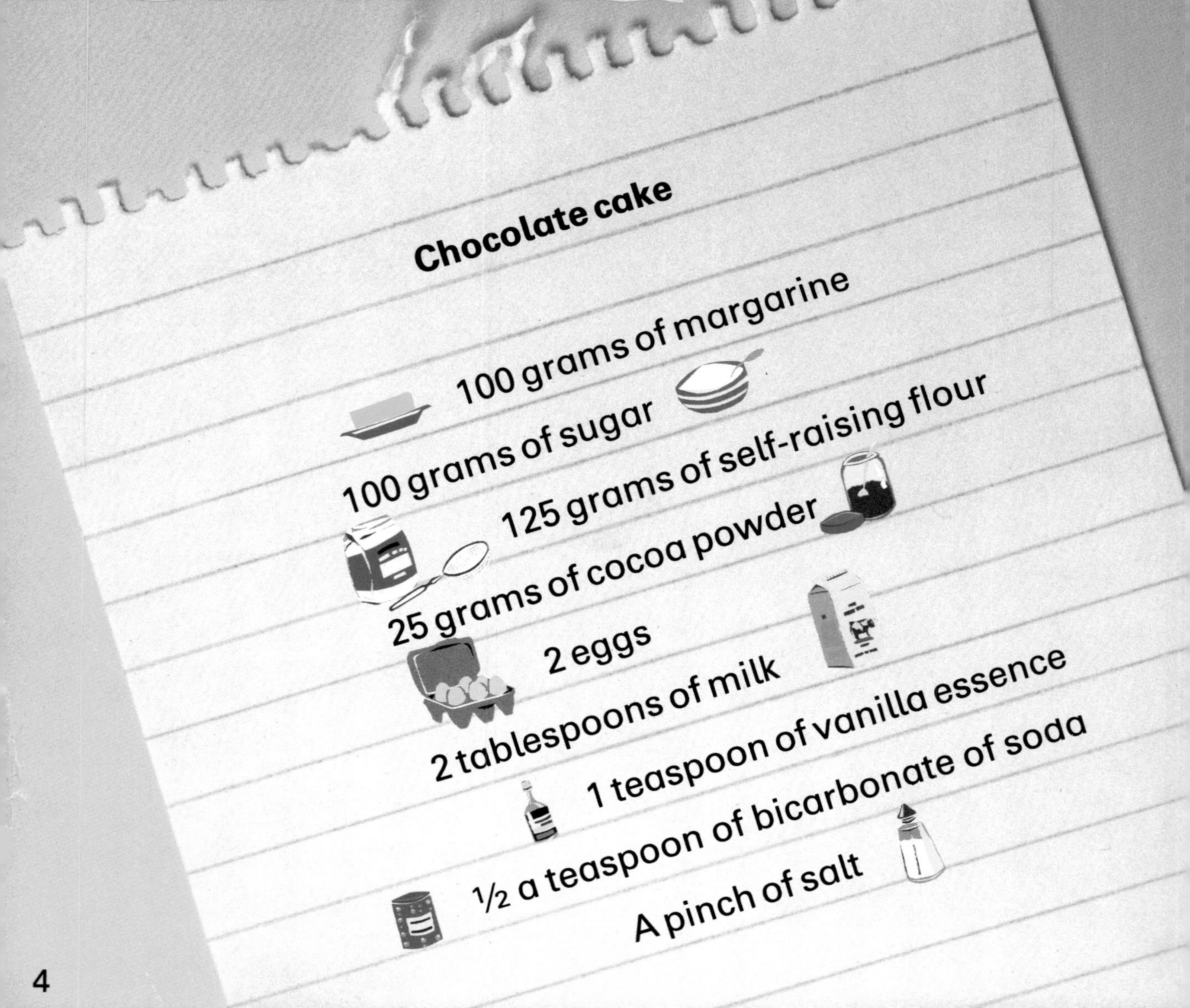

Chocolate cake

100 grams of margarine

100 grams of sugar

125 grams of self-raising flour

25 grams of cocoa powder

2 eggs

2 tablespoons of milk

1 teaspoon of vanilla essence

½ a teaspoon of bicarbonate of soda

A pinch of salt

I measure out the right amount of each thing.

To make my cake...

Sugar

Flour

Milk

Vanilla essence

...I need all these things.

Salt

Margarine

Cocoa powder

Eggs

Bicarbonate of soda

7

Look what happens when I mix
the margarine with the sugar.

When I mix the flour, salt and bicarbonate with the cocoa, it makes a pale brown powder.

What happens to the eggs when I whip them and add the milk?

Now I need to add the
three mixtures together.

I pour the egg mixture into the margarine and sugar. Then I add the vanilla.

When I add the dry things...

...how does the mixture change?

Dad pours the smooth, sticky mixture into the tin...

...and puts the tin into a hot oven.

The heat makes my cake grow.

To help my cake cool down, Dad puts it on a grid.

My cake keeps its shape. It isn't sticky any more.

My cake is full of holes.

My cake has a hard crust. I can spread icing on top.

I'm decorating
my cake.

20

How old am I?

At my party, there's lots of cake for my friends.

What was your birthday cake like?

More things to do

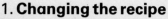

1. Changing the recipe
Now you know how to make a cake, try changing the recipe to see how the cake changes.
Here are some ideas:
— leave out the baking powder or the flour
— put water into the mixture instead of egg
— don't mix the ingredients
— cook the cake for 15 minutes longer
— cook the cake in small bun cases
It's a good idea to change only one thing at a time. Then you can be sure what caused the changes.

2. Cakes and nutrition
Try changing your cake mix to make a healthier cake. You can use less margarine, replace the sugar with a natural sweetener such as dried fruit or honey, or use oats, bran or wholemeal flour instead of some of the self-raising flour. Instead of icing or a cream or jam filling, use a nut cream or paste.

3. Cakes for celebrations
See if you can find out how to make some of the special cakes, such as Christmas cake, gingerbread, Simnel cake or rice cakes, which are used in celebrations all over the world.

Cooking 'My cake'
★For this recipe you need two 7 inch (17.5 cm) sandwich tins. Grease the tins and line them with greaseproof paper, or use non-stick tins.
★Cook the cake at 170°C (325°F), gas mark 3 for about 30-35 minutes.

Find the page

This list shows you where to find some of the ideas in this book.

Notes for parents and teachers

As you share this book with young children, these notes will help you to explain the scientific concepts behind the different activities.

Pages 2, 3   Getting ready for cooking
It's a good idea to involve the children in shopping for the ingredients. In the kitchen, explain the importance of basic hygiene, such as washing hands and putting on a clean apron.

Page 5   Measuring things
It is important to weigh out the right amount of each ingredient. If there is too much or too little of anything, the cake will not cook properly.

Pages 8, 9, 10, 11, 12, 13   Mixing things
When you physically mix things together, the mixing changes the appearance of the original ingredients. They may change colour, for example. This sort of change is reversible.

When the cake is cooked, the ingredients are chemically altered. This change is practically irreversible so you cannot separate out the original ingredients. A chemical change and a physical change are different.

Pages 14, 17   Tins and cake shapes
In the oven, the runny mixture sets into a firm cake, which is the same shape as the tin.

Pages 15, 18   Cooking cakes
The heat in the oven causes a number of chemical changes to take place.

★The bicarbonate of soda dissolves in the liquid from the milk and eggs to form bubbles of a gas, carbon dioxide. There is also some bicarbonate in the baking powder which is in the self-raising flour. (To see the bubbles form, add a teaspoon of baking powder to a glass of water.) If you managed to beat air into the mixture during the mixing process, there will also be bubbles of air in the mixture. As the mixture gets warmer, the bubbles of air and carbon dioxide grow bigger, which makes the cake rise.

★The bubbles become permanent 'holes' when the heat makes the eggs and milk set. (You can see this when you make scrambled eggs.)

★The flour absorbs moisture from the cake mix and turns into a stiff paste. The flour paste makes the mixture stiffer and stronger so the walls around the bubbles don't collapse.

★The sugar and fat hold moisture so the cake is tender.

Page 16   Cooling cakes
The grid allows air to circulate around all sides of the cake so it cools down faster.

Pages 19, 20   Icing and decorating
The icing used for 'My cake' is a butter cream icing but any suitable icing can be chosen.

Page 21   Counting candles
The number of candles on a cake provide a good opportunity to practise counting.

Pages 22, 23   Sharing the cake
In order to explain fractions, a cake can be divided into equal-sized portions. This also encourages the idea of sharing things.